This book is dedicated to Cesare, Massimo and Duggee,
as well as to all the great Golden Retrievers and dogs who will forever remain in our hearts:
Basil, Geronimo, Britt, Bobo, Penny, Rugby, Byron, King, Bridger and Gino.

SPECIAL THANKS:
Thank you Joel Harper, Anna Fontana, Clinica Veterinaria San Martino, Jacquelyn Lazo, Stefano Nada, Karen Coviello, Samantha Nemeth, Genevieve Komorowski, "Zia" Ottavia, Roisin O'Connor, Shauna Langan, Inga Tisonova, Liz Parks, Cary Oliva, Leonardo Travagliati, Kateryna Danyliuk, Miriam Schneider and Nicole for your collective wisdom and support on this project.

ISBN: 979-8-218-46329-8

Library of Congress Control Number: 2024912360

Printed in China on FSC paper

DUGGEE BOOKS
www.DuggeeBooks.com

Life with Duggee

Kathryn Hellwig

Illustrated by Victor Tavares

Buongiorno! I'm Cesare (pronounced Che-zah-rey), and I live in Italy. This story is about my Golden Retriever named Duggee.

I used to be scared of dogs. Some were big and made loud sounds, but all that changed for me after my mom and dad decided to bring a puppy into our family. Let me tell you what happened.

My parents suggested that we adopt a Golden Retriever to help me overcome my fear. When Duggee was two months old, he traveled on a boat from Sicily to reach the mainland of Italy. We could hardly wait to meet him.

With big brown eyes and large ears, Duggee was the cutest, silliest and fluffiest puppy I had ever seen.

As I learned more about him, we became good friends and my fears went away.

Duggee had to learn many things, like I did when I was little. He needed to learn to sit patiently, listen to directions and go to the bathroom outside.

To teach Duggee, we gave him loving reassurance and tasty dog treats.
I love treats too, don't you?

When his big dog teeth were growing, Duggee needed many things to chew on. I tried to make sure he chewed on the right things, like safe wood and chew toys. But sometimes he made mistakes and chewed on the wrong stuff, like shoes… and my toys.

Even though he looked bigger, Duggee was still a puppy the first few years. Young dogs like Duggee are very energetic and don't easily follow directions, so it took a lot of patience and positive feedback to teach him how to be a good dog.

Sometimes, he needed
reminding a gazillion times a day!

When Duggee has a lot of energy, he makes me laugh. However, if he becomes too excited, I have learned to turn around to show him my back so that he knows to calm down.

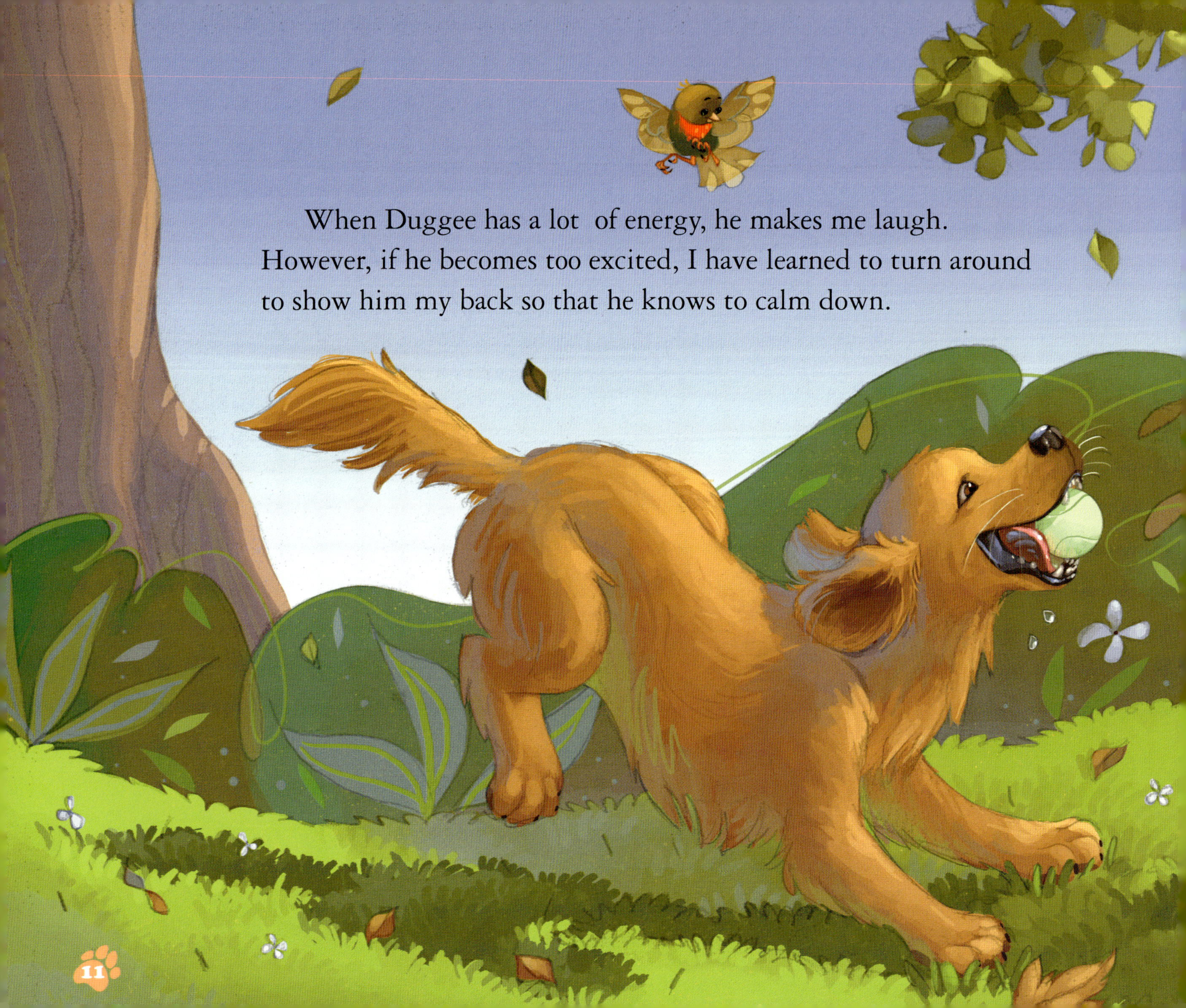

Body language is one of the ways we can communicate with dogs while treating them with kindness.

Duggee has grown into an adult dog who usually knows the difference between right and wrong, so taking him on errands is easier now. As a part of our family, he often joins us so that we can stay together.

Since Duggee arrived, life has never been boring. He always wants to play and makes me laugh. When I'm sad, he helps me feel better with his wet-nose kisses!

Do you want to know what living with a Golden Retriever is like? I'd say Duggee is many things…

Duggee is a super-fast runner and he always tries to steal the ball when we're playing catch.

Duggee loves gelato as much as I do. Gelato is Italian ice cream and it's delicious. He can't have it often because, as with other human treats, his body doesn't digest it easily. A lick every now and then makes him really happy!

Duggee is an excellent dancer! Sometimes we dance to music together in the kitchen.

Duggee is a great hiker. Our family enjoys walking in nature, and Duggee always sniffs out the best path.

Duggee loves to take long naps
at any time of day or night.
He enjoys sleeping in safe, dry spots
near where we are.

Duggee is a funny pirate! He sometimes steals things like socks, pillows and toys, hoping Mom will give him a treat if he returns the treasure! This has actually worked a "few" times.

Duggee will eat anything he can get his paws on. I make sure he gets healthy food, along with some special dog treats. He can't eat some things, so I'm careful with what I feed him. Did you know that chocolate, avocados, onions, garlic, grapes and raisins are some of the foods that can hurt dogs?

As a Golden Retriever, Duggee loves to swim. Whether it's a lake, a pool, the sea, a few puddles, the garden hose or our bathtub, he always wants to play and splash in water.

Duggee even helps with household chores! He loves to clean the floor and the windows with his big, wet tongue.

My dad also thinks he's a great dishwasher.

He is a great friend and protector. Whenever I need a hug or feel worried, Duggee is always close by and makes me feel safe.

I feel protective over him, too, and make sure other kids don't pull his tail or try to ride him like a pony because it would hurt him. We're a good team!

Above all, Duggee is good at spreading love and making friends. Many people ask if they can pet him when we're out together. If you want to pet a dog, be sure to always ask the owner first.

Whether going out for a walk into town or joining our family on the couch, he brings people together and makes us all smile with his sweet, happy face and kind nature.

Life with Duggee truly is “Golden”!

Kathryn Hellwig
the writer

I live with my son, husband and Golden Retriever near a big lake in Northern Italy, not far from the snow-capped Alps. Originally from sunny California, Italy has since become my new home and now our family shares two languages and two cultures. When Duggee joined the fun, we learned a third way of living, dedicated to sharing our time and home with our dog. *Life with Duggee* was written in hopes of spreading Duggee's magic for young readers to enjoy and to support the next generation of responsible and kind pet owners.

Victor Tavares
the illustrator

I live in Brazil with my wife and son. Once, a friend left her two Golden Retrievers, Princess (mom) and Thor (puppy), with us for one month. Thor accidentally hit the glass door with his head. From that day on, whenever Thor was next to that door, Princess would come in front and stretch out her paw to check whether or not the glass was there. They're so much smarter than we think! When I first read *Life with Duggee*, I immediately remembered those magical days. What a wonderful experience it was to illustrate this book.